BEHOLD The FAMILY CIRCUS®

By Bil Keane

THOMAS NELSON PUBLISHERS
Nashville

Published in Nashville, Tennessee, by Thomas Nelson, Inc. and distributed in Canada by Lawson Falle, Ltd., Cambridge, Ontario.

Printed in the United States of America.

Scripture quotations are from THE NEW KING JAMES VERSION of the Bible. Copyright © 1979, 1980, 1982, Thomas Nelson, Inc., Publishers.

ISBN 0-8407-3041-1

1 2 3 4 5 6—93 92 91 90 89

*Behold, children are a gift
of the Lord;
How blessed is the man whose
quiver is full of them;*

PSALM 127:3,5

FOREWORD

For many years "THE FAMILY CIRCUS" has chronicled the day-to-day experiences of the typical American family. In addition to the usual fun, foibles, and frustrations involved with small children, I focus regularly on subjects often side-stepped by cartoonists: God, religion, prayer, church, and heaven.

Some of these cartoons are included here and combined with others that show love, warmth, respect, and concern—traits that are crucial for healthy family life.

Hopefully this book will help you conclude, as I did years ago, that a happy home is as sacred a place as any chapel or cathedral.

Of all the marvelous things created by God, his most precious, tangible, and enduring creation is the family.

Much love to yours,

Bil Keane

"Does our daily bread mean crusts, too?"

"How do you divide your love among four children?"

"I don't divide it. I multiply it."

Blessed are the peacemakers....

5

"Only half of Jeffy's prayers count. He's kneeling on one knee."

"Could the snake really talk, or was it like one of the Muppets?"

"Spring doesn't come till they run out of snow."

"Mommy, what's everybody in heaven say to God when He sneezes?"

"Sarah says her name is in the Bible.
Is Dolly?"

"Can we use this basket, Mommy? We're
playin' church."

"When I get old enough to get married, how will I know which girl to vote for?"

"Cupids are fat babies with no clothes on. Angels wear white bathrobes and circle hats."

10

"I know who those who trespass against us are—Billy and Jeffy and PJ. . . ."

"I'll always love you, Mommy. And I'll always remember your name."

"I'm gonna say my prayers, Daddy. Is there anything you want?"

"My guardian angel f'got to catch me."

12

"Mommy, when I have children, does Billy have to be their uncle?"

"Can you sing me a lovabye?"

"How old do babies hafta get to start bein' boys and girls?"

"Gee, Grandma, you have a lot of thoughts on your wall."

16

"You have to do that when you're married."

"Know what? Washington, Lincoln, and Jesus were all born on holidays."

"Mommy, did you use to be sexy?"

"Those jets will be sorry if God catches them drawing lines on the sky."

21

"They must be growing up. They don't need pushes any more."

"We just figured it out, Mommy. When I'm 19, all four of us will be teenagers at the same time!"

"Was St. Patrick married to Cleopatrick?"

"I'm practicing to be a daddy."

"How am I s'posed to love my neighbor when she didn't even order any of my candy bars?"

"Finders keepers, losers weepers! Saint Anthony said that."

24

26

"I know why we say grace. It's to let our food cool off."

"Mommy's telling us a Bible story 'bout a PUNCHY PILOT."

"How do Easter lilies know what date they hafta have flowers?"

"I'm not asking for anything in particular,
but you could surprise me."

"I like it in church on Easter
when we sing Easter carols."

31

"I hope today is one of the good ol' days Grandma talks about."

"You're not to wear that alarm watch to church ever again."

"That bird did a pretty good job building a nest with no hands, just his mouth."

"We shouldn't pass a beggar by. He could be one of God's angels."

"We're learning our 'Thou
shalt nots.'"

"You hafta listen to me with your eyes,
Daddy. Not just your ears."

"Will I hafta start every day by putting on my clothes for the rest of my life?"

"Did God write the Bible with a word processor, a typewriter, or just a feather and ink?"

"Anytime you're ready, Daddy, I'll be
sitting outside growing older."

"God likes girls best. That's why he
didn't give us whiskers."

"We should be very kind to cats and dogs because they have no words."

"When I get to be an angel, I'm not going to play a harp. I'm going to play the drum."

"Was there an older generation when you were little, Mommy?"

"The outside's almost ready to be morning."

"We can talk to God anytime we want to 'cause he has a toll-free number."

"I'll never understand girls if I live to be 13."

42

"I'm givin' Mommy a spiritual bouquet and usin' my money to get a catcher's mitt."

"Poor Mommy. We get to go to the movies for Mother's Day and she has to stay home."

"Bless Mommy twice
and Daddy twice
and . . ."

"I forgot to say my
prayers last night."

"Who came first—Mother Goose, Mother
Hubbard, or Mother Teresa?"

"He's playing with me now. You can't have him."

"I wish God wouldn't wash the world on Saturdays."

"Look! There's a hole in the sky and I can see a little bit of heaven!"

"Daddy said there'll always be prayer in school as long as they give final exams."

"Is this when God said, 'Let there be cars'?"

"We went to your house yesterday, but we couldn't find you."

"Is it an ad for something, Daddy?"

"What is it we're about to receive?"

49

"First there was God. Next came George Washington, and then Daddy."

"We made a card for Daddy. It says, 'To our father who art in bed . . .'"

"Old people get bent over so they can look
at their grandchildren."

"Can't wait till I'm grown up and I can do
anything I want and not have anything
to worry about."

"You're better than just a father. You're a DADDY!"

"Sometimes I wonder why we bought a seven-room house."

54

"Let's pretend I'm getting married and you guys sing 'Here Comes the Prize.'"

"I'm very tired, Mommy. Will you say good night to Jesus for me and tell him I went to bed?"

"Know why God hasta take some old people? They used up all their birthdays."

"I'm glad you met Mommy, 'cause I wouldn't like not being here."

"We like the sermon part best. That's
when Daddy gets to take PJ outside
and Mommy passes us mints."

"God always turns the lights down when
he's gonna put on a storm."

59

"Why are you kneeling down, Mommy? Are you praying?"

"Know what I like about summer? We don't hafta go indoors to smell dinner cooking."

"Mommy, God's here!"

"Why do they hafta put all the good views on top of hills?"

"We're s'posed to forgive and forget. Well, I forgive Jeffy for eating my candy bar, but I'll never forget it."

"Are you going to bend down here, Grandma, or shall I just hug your legs?"

64

"Mommy, why did God invent 'skeetos'?"

"REAL friends don't hafta keep talking all the time."

"Cameras shrink us so Grandma can carry us around in her wallet."

"When I grow taller than Mommy, I'm going to marry her."

68

69

"This is the best month to go on vacation 'cause August doesn't have any holidays. You hafta make your own."

"You enjoy them even more when you realize this childhood mini-series won't be rerun."

"It's very clear and there aren't any clouds. Why can't we see God up there?"

"If I was borned in the hospital, who came to buy me and bring me home?"

"This is like a church, Mommy. Everyone's whispering."

"The ranger said the river dug the canyon, Mommy, and you said God did it. Who's right?"

"My hand didn't get shooked."

"Dinner's takin' too long to cook, Mommy. We should've brought our microwave oven!"

"Why does God keep flushing the ocean?"

"Wanna wiggle my loose tooth?"

81

"Why was the commercial so long?"

"I sure hope Billy's guardian angel doesn't go on strike."

"Boy! We sure wore this day
to a stub."

"September already! Y'know, Daddy, the
days really fly by when you
get to be seven."

"Grandma looked at the card I made her
and cried 'cause she was touched.
But I didn't touch her, honest!"

"God can't hear you from under
there, Jeffy."

BEFORE YOU CAN
TURN AROUND...

"I really don't care about a moment of silence in school, but I'd like to have one here occasionally."

"Know what's a very pretty word? Grandmother!"

"Why doesn't THAT organist ever play
'Take Me Out to the Ball Game'?"

"This is my favorite place—
inside your hug."

"Hail Mary full of grapes. . . ."

"I need a new football. I don't know if I should
send up a prayer, write a letter to Santa Claus,
or call grandma."

Certainly I was once in love with someone—
with Daddy!"

No, Mommy, not like that. I mean REALLY in
love."

"Won't GOD be surprised!"

"Go to your room! And don't turn on the TV
or the stereo, don't play with your road
racers or the pinball machine . . . on
second thought, go to MY room!"

"Mommy, at weddings, why do they say 'aw-
ful wedded wife'?"

"God hangs fruit on trees so it won't get dirty."

"When I grow up and have kids, how would you like the job as grandparents?"

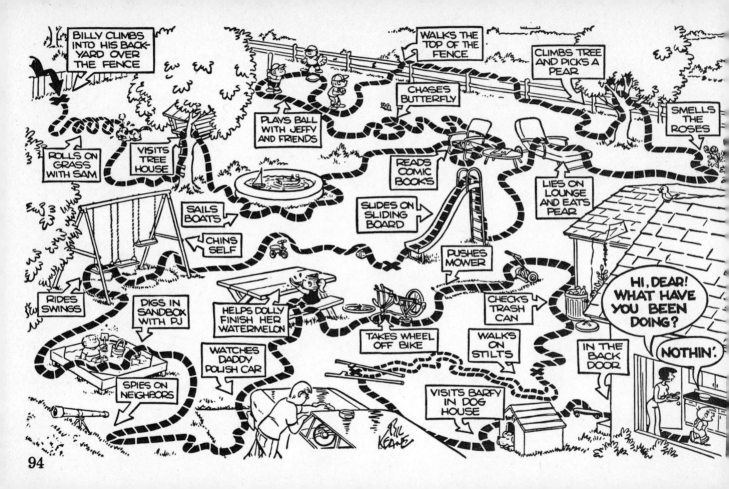

94

"PJ is in there all alone wastin' some of his smiles."

"If I say where the devil lives, will I get in trouble for using a naughty word?"

"That was gonna be our clubhouse, but we ran out of summer."

"And that's the story of Adam and Eve."
"Hey! That would make a good book!"

"Hearing that rain makes me feel friendly, Mommy—as long as it can't get into the house."

"I perform miracles, too. Every morning Daddy says, 'If you make the school bus, it'll be a miracle.'"

"When I grow up, I'm gonna GO places instead of just bein' taken."

"I can hardly wait to go to church tomorrow."

"They're havin' a bake sale after!"

"Have I been good today?"

"When PJ was a tiny baby, why did
the priest at church put him
in a birdbath?"

"They look so sweet and peaceful when they're asleep. You wonder how they could ever yell at us during the day."

"Mommy always says a little prayer when she takes off her shoes. She says, 'Thank God.'"

101

"Trees don't need leaves in the winter 'cause nobody sits under them."

"Daddy said no on the 10-speed bike, so I'm going over his head."

"When the sun shines through those windows, it makes me want to sing 'Somewhere Over the Rainbow.'"

"This is the bestest time of day. Dinners are cookin', kids are bathed, and daddys come home."

"Sure there's a difference between you and me,
Morrie. You're a boy, I'm a girl!"

"We made our own lunch to save you work."

"I thought I was gonna get a computer for my birthday, but I guess my prayer bounced."

"How much did you get, Daddy?"

"He stops you from talking.
He's a husher."

"When we have kids, Grandma won't
be just GRAND. She'll
be GREAT!"

109

"Maybe Granddad and Grandma forgot we
were comin' and went out."

"Hi, Grandma! Remember me?"

"Grandmas are good at hugging because they've had years and years of practice."

"I like it when Grandma and Granddad are here. We can each have a grown-up."

"Daddys take you for runs and drives, but
granddads take you for walks."

"We're playing ark."

113

"Who crayoned your windows?"

"Father Forrest said, 'As you live, so shall you die.' I'll bet Billy dies in a messy room."

114

"Swaddling clothes are diapers and booties—
stuff like that."

"Behold! It snoweth!"

"That angel's name is Harold."

"And Joseph couldn't get them a room 'cause all the motels were overbooked."

"God gift-wrapped the world!"

"Arnold Roth is lucky. His mother's Christmas an
his father's Hanukkah."

"I'm not dirty. I just look
lived in."

"Betcha Jesus missed out on a ton
of presents 'cause his birthday
and Christmas were on the
very same day."

"Stop it, PJ. Don't you know this is the season to be jolly?"

"Dear Santa, bless Mommy and Daddy and . . . I mean, Dear God, bless Mommy and . . ."

"Was the drummer boy the only little kid invited to baby Jesus' birthday party?"

"Wish I could keep that red light on in my room all year 'cause it makes me warm and happy."

"Burning candles make you feel quiet. That's why they have them in church."

". . . Holy instant so tender and mild. . . ."

"Jeffy tried to kiss Santa's ring."

"My brother is one of the wise guys."

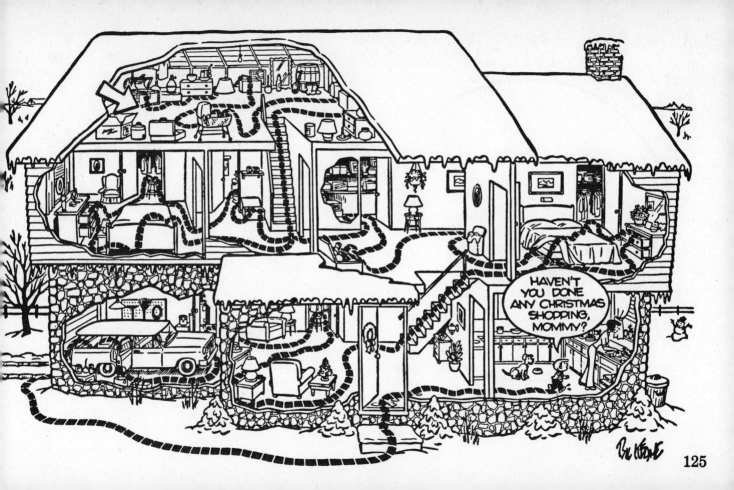

125

"Here he is! The star
of Bethlehem!"

"They won't know it till they're grown,
but their BEST gifts are the memories
they're making."

"There's one other gift for you, Daddy—over here under the mistletoe."

"Finally! Peace on earth! The batteries are worn out!"